The Night Before Christmas

A Mariposa Inspirations publication

Adapted from the original poem by Major Henry Livingston, Jr.
Account of a Visit from St. Nicholas
public domain

The Night Before Christmas © 2025, Tim & Becca Bartel

ISBN: 978-0-9769242-3-4

The Night Before Christmas

Adapted by Tim & Becca Bartel

For our grandchildren:
Noah, Matthew, Eva and Isaac

'Twas the night before Christmas,
when all through the house
not a creature was stirring,
not even a mouse;

Some cookies and milk
we set up by a chair,
in hope that Saint Nicholas
soon would be there;

The kids were asleep,
sprawled out in their beds,
while visions of video games
raced in their heads;

Dad in his sleep mask
and I my silk cap,
hoping for more than
a one~hour nap;

When out on the lawn
there arose such a clatter,
I jumped out of bed
to see what was the matter;

Straight to the window,
I flew in a flash,
tore back the curtains,
wiped frost from the glass;

The moon shining bright
on the new~fallen snow,
lit everything up,
like a jumbotron's glow.

When, what to my wondering
eyes should appear,
but a rugged old sleigh,
and eight tiny reindeer;

With a little old driver,
so lively and quick,
I knew in a moment
it must be Saint Nick.

As snowflakes whirl

when the winter winds sigh,

or drones in formation

rise up to the sky.

Just so, to the housetop

the reindeer they flew,

with the sled full of toys,

and Santa Claus too;

And then, in a twinkling,

I heard on the roof

the prancing and pawing

of each little hoof;

Down the chimney slid Santa,
with hardly a stall,
sticking the landing,
with three points and all;

He was dressed all in fur,
from his head to his foot,
yet he left not a trail
of ashes or soot;

A bundle of toys

he let down from his back,

and he looked like a hiker,

just opening his pack;

He peered through spectacles,
so perfectly round,
checking names on a list
that unrolled to the ground;

His eyes—how they twinkled!
His dimples, how merry!
His cheeks were like roses,
his nose like a cherry!

His handlebar 'stache
curved up like a bow,
and the beard on his chin
was as white as the snow;

He had a broad face
and a little round belly
that shook when he laughed,
like a bowlful of jelly;

He was chubby and plump,
and elfishly odd,
Papa chuckled to see him,
despite his dad bod;

A selfie I took,
with my phone I held out,
giving me proof
that no one would doubt;

He spoke not a word
as he wrapped up his work,
putting out presents,
then turned with a smirk;

And laying his finger
aside of his nose,
and giving a wink,
up the chimney he rose;

He sprang to his sleigh,
pulled back on the reins,
as he whistled and shouted
and called them by name:

"Now, Dasher! now, Dancer!
now, Prancer and Vixen!
On, Comet! on, Cupid!
on, Donder and Blitzen!

To the top of the porch!
to the top of the wall!
Now dash away! dash away!
dash away all!"

He adjusted his cap,
to his team gave a whistle,
and away they all flew,
like a rocket or missile.

But I heard him exclaim,
as he drove out of sight,
"Merry Christmas to all,
and to all a good night!"

The End

Accounnt of A Visit from St. Nicholas
By Henry Livingston, Jr.

'Twas the night before Christmas, when all thro' the house,

Not a creature was stirring, not even a mouse;

The stockings were hung by the chimney with care,

In hopes that St. Nicholas soon would be there;

The children were nestled all snug in their beds,

While visions of sugar plums danc'd in their heads,

And Mama in her 'kerchief, and I in my cap,

Had just settled our brains for a long winter's nap —

When out on the lawn there arose such a clatter,

I sprang from the bed to see what was the matter.

Away to the window I flew like a flash,

Tore open the shutters, and threw up the sash.

The moon on the breast of the new fallen snow,

Gave the lustre of mid~day to objects below;

When, what to my wondering eyes should appear,

But a miniature sleigh, and eight tiny rein~deer,

With a little old driver, so lively and quick,

I knew in a moment it must be St. Nick.

More rapid than eagles his coursers they came,

And he whistled, and shouted, and call'd them by name:

"Now! Dasher, now! Dancer, now! Prancer, and Vixen,

"On! Comet, on! Cupid, on! Dunder and Blixem;

"To the top of the porch! to the top of the wall!

"Now dash away! dash away! dash away all!"

As dry leaves before the wild hurricane fly,

When they meet with an obstacle, mount to the sky;

So up to the house~top the coursers they flew,

With the sleigh full of Toys — and St. Nicholas too:

And then in a twinkling, I heard on the roof
The prancing and pawing of each little hoof.
As I drew in my head, and was turning around,
Down the chimney St. Nicholas came with a bound:
He was dress'd all in fur, from his head to his foot,
And his clothes were all tarnish'd with ashes and soot;
A bundle of toys was flung on his back,
And he look'd like a peddler just opening his pack:
His eyes — how they twinkled! his dimples how merry,
His cheeks were like roses, his nose like a cherry;
His droll little mouth was drawn up like a bow.
And the beard of his chin was as white as the snow;
The stump of a pipe he held tight in his teeth,
And the smoke it encircled his head like a wreath.

He had a broad face, and a little round belly
That shook when he laugh'd, like a bowl full of jelly:
He was chubby and plump, a right jolly old elf,
And I laugh'd when I saw him in spite of myself;
A wink of his eye and a twist of his head
Soon gave me to know I had nothing to dread.
He spoke not a word, but went straight to his work,
And fill'd all the stockings; then turn'd with a jerk,
And laying his finger aside of his nose
And giving a nod, up the chimney he rose.
He sprung to his sleigh, to his team gave a whistle,
And away they all flew, like the down of a thistle:
But I heard him exclaim, ere he drove out of sight —
Happy Christmas to all, and to all a good night.

Illustrated by Babzy the Elf

www.ingramcontent.com/pod-product-compliance
Lightning Source LLC
Chambersburg PA
CBRC101828090426
42811CB00024B/1925